George William Bagby

Canal Reminiscences

Recollections of Travel in the Old Days on the James River & Kanawha

Canal

George William Bagby

Canal Reminiscences
Recollections of Travel in the Old Days on the James River & Kanawha Canal

ISBN/EAN: 9783337210663

Printed in Europe, USA, Canada, Australia, Japan

Cover: Foto ©Andreas Hilbeck / pixelio.de

More available books at **www.hansebooks.com**

CANAL

REMINISCENCES:

Recollections of Travel in the Old Days

ON THE

James River & Kanawha Canal.

BY

GEORGE W. BAGBY.

RICHMOND:

WEST, JOHNSTON & CO., PUBLISHERS.

1879.

Printed by
Whittet & Shepperson,
Richmond, Va.

Preface.

My first thought was to print these reminiscences in a newspaper. But our papers are unable to pay for contributions. It was not so in the former days. Well do I remember when the *Dispatch* cheerfully gave me its dollars, not merely for stories and sketches, but for trifles like the " *Weekly Rekord uv amewsments*," which I then kept, and which seemed to please our good people of Richmond, who were then doing so well in business that they were easily pleased. And truly in those times they were a liberal, open-hearted set. So would they be now were they able.

Will we ever see good times and plenty of money again? I think so. And yet often I get very blue, apprehending still greater business troubles, culmi-

nating in I know not what of civil disaster. It is
touching to me, going around, as I have had to do a
great deal of late, among our business men, to see
. their sad faces, and yet their evident anxiety in the
midst of worries and cares, to help one who is even
worse off than themselves. We have good stock
here—men who would honor any city in the land,
and who make up a community in which it is a
pleasure to live. Here and there you find one, two,
or three close-fisted fellows, who dodge you for fear
you will ask them for something. That is to their
credit, for it shows that they have feeling and a sense
of shame. And again you meet positive brutes, who
are not merely stingy and mean, but ill-mannered
and under-bred to boot. But these serve as-foils to
set off their better brethren to more advantage; and
I, for one, am not the man to abuse stingy people.
They have one magnificent trait to counterpoise
their littleness—they pay their debts, and pay them
promptly. So, take it all in all, Richmond is about

as good a place to live in as a man will find on this globe, as I have learned by playing book-canvasser, —an excellent school for the study of men.

But shall we see better times? Why, yes, surely. They have begun already in Troy, N. Y., the papers say. And I verily believe the railway, which is to take the place of the canal, will do more than all things else to bring back work for all and money for all of us in our fair city of Richmond. Let us at least hope so. And with that hope in view, I trust that these reminiscences of an obsolescent mode of travel—which may have been delightful, but certainly was not rapid—will give a few moments of pleasure to the friends of the publishers and of the writer.

G. W. B.

Canal Reminiscences.

AMONG my earliest recollections is a trip from Cumberland County to Lynchburg, in 1835, or thereabouts. As the stage approached Glover's tavern in Appomattox county, sounds as of a cannonade aroused my childish curiosity to a high pitch. I had been reading Parley's History of America, and this must be the noise of actual battle. Yes; the war against the hateful Britishers must have broken out again. Would the stage carry us within range of the cannon balls? Yes, and presently the red-coats would come swarming out of the woods. And—and—Gen. Washington was dead; I was certain of that; what would become of us? I was terribly excited, but afraid to ask questions. Perhaps I was scared.

Would they kill an unarmed boy, sitting peacably in a stage coach? Of course they would; Britishers will do anything! Then they will have to shoot a couple of men first;—and I squeezed still closer between them.

My relief and my disappointment were equally great, when a casual remark unfolded the fact that the noise which so excited me was only the "blasting of rock on the Jeems and Kanawha Canell." What was "blasting of rock?"

What was a "canell?" and, above all, what manner of thing was a "Jeems and Kanawha Canell?" Was it alive?

I think it was; more alive than it has ever been since, except for the first few years after it was opened.

Those were the "good old days" of batteaux,—picturesque craft that charmed my young eyes more than all the gondolas of Venice would do now. True, they consumed a week in getting from Lynchburg to Richmond, and ten days in returning against the stream, but what of that? Time was abundant in those days. It was made for slaves, and we had the slaves. A batteau on the water was more than a match for the best four or six horse bell-team that ever rolled over the red clay of Bedford, brindle dog and tar-bucket included.

Fleets of these batteaux used to be moored on the river bank near where the depot of the Virginia and Tennessee Railroad now stands; and many years after the "Jeems and Kanawha" was finished, one of them used to haunt the mouth of Blackwater creek above the toll-bridge, a relic of departed glory. For if ever man gloried in his calling,—the negro batteau-man was that man. His was a hardy calling, demanding skill, courage and strength in a high degree. I can see him now striding the plank that ran along the gunwale to afford him footing, his long iron-shod pole trailing in the water behind him. Now he turns, and after one or two ineffectual efforts to get his pole fixed in the rocky bottom of the river, secures his

purchase, adjusts the upper part of the pole to the pad
at his shoulder, bends to his task, and the long,
but not ungraceful bark mounts the rapids like
a sea-bird breasting the storm. His companion
on the other side plies the pole with equal ardor,
and between the two the boat bravely surmounts every
obstacle, be it rocks, rapids, quicksands, hammocks,
what not. A third negro at the stern held the
mighty oar that served as a rudder. A stalwart,
jolly, courageous set they were, plying the pole all
day, hauling in to shore at night under the friendly
shade of a mighty sycamore, to rest, to eat, to play
the banjo, and to snatch a few hours of profound,
blissful sleep.

The up-cargo, consisting of sacks of salt, bags of
coffee, barrels of sugar, molasses and whiskey, af-
forded good pickings. These sturdy fellows lived
well, I promise you, and if they stole a little, why,
what was their petty thieving compared to the enor-
mous pillage of the modern sugar refiner and the

crooked-whiskey distiller? They lived well. Their
cook's galley was a little dirt thrown between the
ribs of the boat at the stern, with an awning on oc-
casion to keep off the rain, and what they didn't eat
wasn't worth eating. Fish of the very best, both
salt and fresh, chickens, eggs, milk and the invinci-
ble, never-satisfying ash-cake and fried bacon. I see
the frying-pan, I smell the meat, the fish, the Rio
coffee!—I want the batteau back again, aye! and the
brave, light-hearted slave to boot. What did he
know about the State debt? There was no State
debt to speak of. Greenbacks? Bless, you! the
Farmers Bank of Virginia was living and breathing,
and its money was good enough for a king. Readjustment, funding bill, tax-receivable coupons—
where were all these worries then? I think if we
had known they were coming, we would have stuck
to the batteaux and never dammed the river. Why,
shad used to run to Lynchburg! The world was
merry, butter-milk was abundant; Lynchburg a lad,

Richmond a mere youth, and the great "Jeems and Kanawha canell" was going to—oh! it was going to do everything.

This was forty years ago and more, mark you.

In 1838, I made my first trip to Richmond. What visions of grandeur filled my youthful imagination! That eventually I should get to be a man seemed probable, but that I should ever be big enough to live, actually live, in the vast metropolis, was beyond my dreams. For I believed fully that men were proportioned to the size of the cities they lived in. I had seen a man named Hatcher from Cartersville, who was near about the size of the average man in Lynchburg, but as I had never seen Cartersville, I concluded, naturally enough, that Cartersville must be equal in population. Which may be the fact, for I have never yet seen Cartersville, though I have been to Warminster, and once came near passing through Bent-Creek.

I went by stage.

It took two days to make the trip, yet no one com-
plained, although there were many Methodist minis-
ters aboard. Bro. Lafferty had not been born. I
thought it simply glorious. There was an unnatural preponderance of preacher to boy,—nine of
preacher to one of boy. That boy did not take a
leading part in the conversation. He looked out of
the window, and thought much about Richmond.
And what a wonderful world it was! So many trees,
such nice rocks, and pretty ruts in the red clay; such
glorious taverns, and men with red noses; such
splendid horses, a fresh team every ten miles, and
an elegant smell of leather, proceeding from the coach,
prevailing everywhere as we bowled merrily along.
And then the stage horn. Let me not speak of it,
lest Thomas and his orchestra hang their heads for
very shame. I wish somebody would tell me where
we stopped the first night, for I have quite forgotten.
Any how, it was on the left-hand side coming down,

and I rather think on the brow of a little hill. I
know we got up mighty soon the next morning.

We drew up at the Eagle hotel in Richmond.
Here again words, and time too, fail me. All the
cities on earth packed into one wouldn't look as big
and fine to me now as Main street did then. If
things shrink so in the brief space of a life-time,
what would be the general appearance, say of Peters-
burg, if one should live a million or so of years? This
is an interesting question, which you may discuss
with yourself, dear reader.

Going northward, I remained a year or two, and
on my return the "canell" was finished. I had seen
bigger places than Richmond, but had yet to have
my first experience of canal travelling. The packet-
landing at the foot of Eighth street presented a scene
of great activity. Passengers on foot and in vehicles
continued to arrive up to the moment of starting. I
took a peep at the cabin, wondering much how all
the passengers were to be accommodated for the

night, saw how nicely the baggage was stored away on deck, admired the smart waiters, and picked up a deal of information generally. I became acquainted with the names of Edmond & Davenport in Richmond, and Boyd, Edmond & Davenport in Lynchburg, the owners of the'packet-line, and thought to myself, "What immensely rich men they must be! Why, these boats cost ten times as much as a stage-coach, and I am told they have them by the dozen."

At last we were off, slowly pushed along under the bridge on Seventh street; then the horses were hitched; then slowly along till we passed the crowd of boats near the city, until at length, with a lively jerk as the horses fell into a trot, away we went, the cut-water throwing up the spray as we rounded the Penitentiary hill, and the passengers lingering on deck to get a last look at the fair city of Richmond, lighted by the pale rays of the setting sun.

As the shadows deepened, everybody went below. There was always a crowd in those days, but it was a

crowd for the most part of our best people, and no
one minded it. I was little, and it took little room
to accommodate me. Everything seemed as cozy
and comfortable as heart could wish. I brought to
the table,—an excellent one it was,—a school boy's ap-
petite, sharpened by travel, and thought it was "just
splendid."

Supper over, the men went on deck to smoke,
while the ladies busied themselves with draughts or
backgammon, with conversation or with books. But
not for long. The curtains which separated the
female from the male department were soon drawn,
in order that the steward and his aids might make
ready the berths. These were three deep, "lower,"
"middle" and "upper;" and great was the desire on
the part of the men not to be consigned to the
"upper." Being light as a cork, I rose naturally to
the top, clambering thither by the leathern straps with
the agility of a monkey, and enjoying as best I might
the trampling overhead whenever we approached

a lock. I didn't mind this much, but when the fellow who had snubbed the boat jumped down about four feet, right on my head as it were, it was pretty severe. Still I slept the sleep of youth. We all went to bed early. A few lingered, talking in low tones; and way-passengers, in case there was a crowd, were dumped upon mattresses, placed on the dining tables.

The lamp shed a dim light over the sleepers, and all went well till some one—and there always was some one—began to snore. *Sn-a-a aw !—aw-aw-poof!* They would turn uneasily and try to compose themselves to slumber again. No use. *Sn-a-a-aw— poof!* "D —— that fellow! Chunk him in the ribs, somebody, and make him turn over. Is this thing to go on forever? Gentlemen, are you going to stand this all night? If you are, I am not. I am going to get up and dress. Who is he anyhow? No gentleman would or could snore in that way."

After a while silence would be restored, and all

would drop off to sleep again, except the little fellow in the upper berth, who lying there would listen to the *trahn-ahn-ahn-ahn* of the packet-horn as we drew nigh the locks. How mournfully it sounded in the night! what a doleful thing it is at best, and how different from the stage-horn with its cheery, ringing notes! The difference in the horns marks the difference in the two eras of travel; not that the canal period is doleful—I would not say that, but it is less bright than the period of the stage-coach.

To this day you have only to say within my hearing *trahn-ahn-ahn*, to bring back the canal epoch. I can see the whole thing down to the snubbing post with its deep grooves which the heavy rope had worn. Indeed, I think I could snub a boat myself with very little practice, if the man on deck would say "*hup!*" to the horses at the proper time.

We turned out early in the morning, and had precious little room for dressing. But that was no hardship to me, who had just emerged from a big boarding school dormitory. Still, I must say, being now a grown and oldish man, that I would not like to live and sleep and dress for twenty or thirty years in the cabin of a canal-packet. The ceremony of ablution was performed in a primitive fashion. There were the tin basins, the big tin dipper with the long wooden handle. I feel it vibrating in the water now, and the water a little muddy generally; and there were the towels, a big one on a roller, and the little ones in a pile, and all of them wet. These were discomforts, it is true, but, pshaw! one good, big, long, deep draught of pure, fresh morning air—one glimpse of the roseate flush above the wooded hills of the James, one look at the dew besprent bushes and vines along the canal bank—one sweet caress of dear mother nature in her morning robes, made ample compensation for them all. Breakfast was soon served, and all the more enjoyed in consequence of an hour's fasting on deck; the sun came out in all his splendor ; the day was fairly set in, and with it there was abun-

dant leisure to enjoy the scenery, that grew more and
more captivating as we rose, lock after lock, into the
rock-bound eminences of the upper James.   This
scenery I will not attempt to describe, for time has
sadly dimmed it in my recollection.   The wealth of
the lowlands, and the upland beauty must be seen as
I have seen them, in the day of their prime, to be enjoyed.

The perfect cultivation, the abundance, the elegance,
the ducal splendor, one might almost say, of the great
estates that lay along the canal in the old days have
passed away in a great measure.   Here were gentlemen, not merely refined and educated, fitted to dis-
play a royal hospitality and to devote their leisure
to the study of the art and practice of government,
but they were great and greatly successful farmers
as well.   The land teemed with all manner of pro-
ducts, cereals, fruits, what not ! negroes by the hun-
dreds and the thousands, under wise direction, gen-
tle but firm control, plied the hoe to good purpose.

There was enough and to spare for all—to spare?
aye! to bestow with glad and lavish hospitality. A
mighty change has been wrought. What that change
is in all of its effects mine eyes have happily been
spared the seeing; but well I remember—I can never
forget—how from time to time the boat would stop
at one of these estates, and the planter, his wife, his
daughters, and the guests that were going home with
him, would be met by those who had remained behind, and how joyous the greetings were! It was a
bright and happy scene, and it continually repeated
itself as we went onward.

In fine summer weather, the passengers, male and
female, stayed most of the time on deck, where there
was a great deal to interest, and naught to mar
the happiness, except the oft-repeated warning,
"*braidge!*" "*low braidge!*" No well-regulated
packet-hand was ever allowed to say plain "bridge;"
that was an etymological crime in canal ethics. For
the men, this on-deck existence was especially de-

lightful; it is *such* a comfort to spit plump into the water without the trouble of feeling around with your head, in the midst of a political discussion, for the spittoon.

As for me, I often went below, to devour Dickens's earlier novels, which were then appearing in rapid succession. But, drawn by the charm of the scenery, I would often drop my book and go back on deck again. There was an islet in the river—where, exactly, I cannot tell—which had a beauty of its own for me, because from the moment I first saw it, my purpose was to make it the scene of a romance, when I got to be a great big man, old enough to write for the papers. There is a point at which the passengers would get off, and taking a near cut across the hills, would stretch their legs with a mile or two of walking. It was unmanly, I held, to miss that. Apropos of scenery, I must not forget the haunted house near Manchester, which was pointed out soon after we left Richmond, and filled me with awe; for

though I said I did not believe in ghosts, I did. The
ruined mill, a mile or two further, on was always an
object of melancholy interest to me; and of all the
locks from Lynchburg down, the Three-Mile Locks
pleased me most. It is a pretty place, as every one
will own on seeing it. It was so clean and green,
and white and thrifty-looking. To me it was simply
beautiful. I wanted to live there; I ought to have
lived there. I was built for a lock-keeper—have that
exact moral and mental shape. Ah! to own your
own negro, who would do all the drudgery of opening the gates. Occasionally you would go through
the form of putting your shoulder to the huge
wooden levers, if that is what they call them, by
which the gates are opened: to own your own negro
and live and die calmly at a lock! What more
could the soul ask? I do think that the finest picture extant of peace and contentment—a little ab-
normal, perhaps, in the position of the animal—is
that of a sick mule looking out of the window of a

canal freight-boat. And that you could see every day
from the porch of your cottage, if you lived at a
lock, owned your own negro, and there was no
great rush of business on the canal, (and there sel-
dom was) on the "Jeems and Kanawhy," as old
Capt. Sam Wyatt always called it, leaving out the
word "canal," for that was understood. Yes, one
ought to live as a pure and resigned lock-keeper, if
one would be blest, really blest.

Now that I am on the back track, let me add that,
however bold and picturesque the cliffs and bluffs
near Lynchburg and beyond, there was nothing from
one end the canal to the other to compare with the
first sight of Richmond, when, rounding a corner not
far from Hollywood, it burst full upon the vision, its
capitol, its spires, its happy homes, flushed with the
red glow of evening. And what it looked to be, it
was. Its interior, far from belieing its exterior,
surpassed it. The world over, there is no lovelier
site for a city; and the world over there was no city

that quite equalled it in the charm of its hospitality, its refinement, its intelligence, its cordial welcome to strangers. Few of its inhabitants were very rich, fewer still were very poor. But I must not dwell on this. Beautiful city! beautiful city! you may grow to be as populous as London, and sure no one wishes you greater prosperity than I, but grow as you may, you can never be happier than you were in the days whereof I speak. How your picture comes back to me, softened by time, glorified by all the tender, glowing tints of memory. Around you now is the added glory of history, a defence almost unrivalled in the annals of warfare; but for me there is something even brighter than historic fame, a hue derived only from the heaven of memory. In my childhood, when all things were beautified by the unclouded light of "the young soul wandering here in nature," I saw you in your youth, full of hope, full of promise, full of all those gracious influences which made your State greatest among all her sisters, and which seemed concentrated in yourself. Be your maturity what it may, it can never be brighter than this.

To return to the boat. All the scenery in the world—rocks that Salvator would love to paint, and skies that Claude could never limn—all the facilities for spitting that earth affords, avail not to keep a Virginian away from a julep on a hot summer day. From time to time he would descend from the deck of the packet and refresh himself. The bar was small, but vigorous and healthy. I was then in the lemonade stage of boyhood, and it was not until many years afterwards that I rose through porterees and claret-punches to the sublimity of the sherry cobbler, and discovered that the packet bar supplied genuine Havana cigars at fourpence-ha'penny. Why, eggs were but sixpence a dozen on the canal bank, and the national debt wouldn't have filled a tea-cup. Internal revenue was unknown; the coupons receivable for taxes inconceivable, and forcible readjustment a thing undreamt of in Virginian philosophy. Mr. Mallock's pregnant question, "Is life worth living?" was answered very satisfactorily, methought, as I watched the Virginians at their juleps: "Gentlemen, your very good health;" "Colonel, my respects to you;" "My regards, Judge. When shall I see you again at my house? Can't you stop now and stay a little while, if it is only a week or two?" "Sam," (to the bar-keeper,) "duplicate these drinks."

How they smacked their lips; how hot the talk on politics became; and how pernicious this example of drinking in public was to the boy who looked on! Oh! yes; and if you expect your son to go through life without bad examples set him by his elders in a thousand ways, you must take him to another sphere. Still, the fewer bad examples the better, and you, at least, need not set them.

Travelling always with my father, who was a merchant, it was natural that I should become acquainted with merchants. But I remember very few of them.

Mr. Daniel H. London, who was a character, and
Mr. Fleming James, who often visited his estate in
Roanoke, and was more of a character than London,
I recall quite vividly. I remember, too, Mr. Francis B.
Deane, who was always talking about Mobjack Bay,
and who was yet to build the Langhorne Foundry
in Lynchburg. I thought if I could just see Mob-
jack Bay, I would be happy. According to Mr.
Deane, and I agreed with him, there ought by this
time to have been a great city on Mobjack Bay. I
saw Mobjack Bay last summer, and was happy.
Any man who goes to Gloucester will be happy.
More marked than all of these characters was Major
Yancey, of Buckingham, "the wheel-horse of De-
mocracy," he was called; Tim. Rives, of Prince
George, whose face, some said, resembled the inside
of a gunlock, being the war-horse. Major Y.'s stout
figure, florid face, and animated, forcible manner,
come back with some distinctness; and there are
other forms, but they are merely outlines barely dis-

cernible. So pass away men who, in their day, were names and powers—shadows gone into shadow-land, leaving but a dim print upon a few brains, which in time will soon flit away.

Arrived in Lynchburg, the effect of the canal was soon seen in the array of freight boats, the activity and bustle at the packet landing. New names and new faces, from the canal region of New York, most likely, were seen and heard. I became acquainted with the family of Capt. Huntley, who commanded one of the boats, and was for some years quite intimate with his pretty daughters, Lizzie, Harriet and Emma. Capt. H. lived on Church street, next door to the Reformed, or as it was then called, the Radical Methodist Church, and nearly opposite to Mr. Peleg Seabury. He was for a time connected in some way with the Exchange hotel, but removed with his family to Cincinnati, since when I have never but once heard of them. Where are they all, I wonder? Then, there was a Mr. Watson, who

lived with Boyd, Edmond & Davenport, married
first a Miss ——, and afterwards, Mrs. Christian,
went into the tobacco business in Brooklyn, then
disappeared, leaving no trace, not the slightest. Then
there was a rare fellow, Charles Buckley, who lived
in the same store with Watson, had a fine voice, and
without a particle of religion in the ordinary sense,
loved dearly to sing at revivals. I went with him ;
we took back seats, and sang with great fer-
vor. This was at night. Besides Captain Huntley, I remember among the captains of a later
date, Captain Jack Yeatman; and at a date
still later his brother, Captain C. E. Yeatman,
both of whom are still living. There was still
another captain whose name was Love—— something, a very handsome man ; and these are all.

In 1849, having graduated in Philadelphia, I
made one of my last through-trips on the canal, the
happy owner of a diploma in a green tin case, and
the utterly miserable possessor of a dyspepsia which

threatened my life. I enjoyed the night on deck, sick as I was. The owl's "long hoot," the "plaintive cry of the whippoorwill;" the melody—for it is by association a melody, which the Greeks have but travestied with their *brek-ke-ex, ko-ex*—of the frogs, the mingled hum of insect life, the "stilly sound" of inanimate nature, the soft respiration of sleeping earth, and above all, the ineffable glory of the stars. Oh! heaven of heavens, into which the sick boy, lying alone on deck, then looked, has thy charm fled, too, with so many other charms? Have thirty years of suffering, of thought, of book-reading, brougth only the unconsoling knowledge, that yonder twinkling sparks of far-off fire are not lamps that light the portals of the palace of the King and Father, but suns like our sun, surrounded by earths full of woe and doubt like our own ; and that heaven, if heaven there be, is not in the sky ; not in space, vast as it is ; not in time, endless though it be—where then? "Near thee, in thy heart!" Who feels this, who

will say this of himself? Away thou gray-haired,
sunken-cheeked sceptic, away! Come back to me,
come back to me, wan youth; there on that deck,
with the treasure of thy faith, thy trust in men, thy
worship of womankind, thy hope, that sickness
could not chill, in the sweet possibilities of life.
Come back to me!—'Tis a vain cry. The youth lies
there on the packet's deck, looking upward to the
stars, and he will not return.

The trip in 1849 was a dreary one until there came
aboard a dear lady friend of mine who had recently
been married. I had not had a good honest talk
with a girl for eighteen solid—I think I had better
say long, (we always say long when speaking of the
war)—"fo' long years!"—I have heard it a thousand
times—for eighteen long months, and you may im-
agine how I enjoyed the conversation with my friend.
She wasn't very pretty, and her husband was a Louisa
man; but her talk, full of good heart and good sense,
put new life into me. One other through trip, the

very last, I made in 1851. On my return in 1853, I went by rail as far as Farmville, and thence by stage to Lynchburg; so that, for purposes of through travel, the canal lasted, one may say, only ten or a dozen years. And now the canal, after a fair and costly trial, is to give place to the rail, and I, in common with the great body of Virginians, am heartily glad of it. It has served its purpose well enough, perhaps, for its day and generation. The world has passed by it, as it has passed by slavery. Henceforth Virginia must prove her metal in the front of steam, electricity, and possibly mightier forces still. If she can't hold her own in their presence, she must go under. I believe she will hold her own; these very forces will help her. The dream of the great canal to the Ohio, with its-nine mile tunnel, costing fifty or more millions, furnished by the general government, and revolutionizing the commerce of the United States, much as the discovery of America and opening of the Suez canal revolutionized the commerce of the world, must be abandoned along with other dreams.

One cannot withhold admiration from President Johnston and other officers of the canal, who made such a manful struggle to save it. But who can war against the elements? Nature herself, imitating man, seems to have taken special delight in kicking the canal after it was down. So it must go. Well, let it go. It knew Virginia in her palmiest days and it crushed the stage coach; isn't that glory enough? I think it is. But I can't help feeling sorry for the bull frogs; there must be a good many of them between here and Lexington. What will become of them, I wonder? They will follow their predecessors, the batteaux; and their pale, green ghosts, seated on the prows of shadowy barges, will be heard piping the roundelays of long-departed joys.

Farewell canal, frogs, musk-rats, mules, packet-horns and all, a long farewell. Welcome the rail along the winding valleys of the James. Wake up,

Fluvanna! Arise, old Buckingham! Exalt thyself,
O Goochland! And thou, O Powhatan, be not
afraid nor shame-faced any longer, but raise thy
Ebenezer freely, for the day of thy redemption is at
hand. Willis J. Dance shall rejoice; yea, Wm. Pope
Dabney shall be exceeding glad. And all hail our
long lost brother! come to these empty, aching, arms,
dear Lynch's Ferry !

I have always thought that the unnatural separation between Lynchburg and Richmond was the
source of all our troubles. In some way, not entirely
clear to me, it brought on the late war, and it will
bring on another, if a reunion between the two cities
does not soon take place. Baltimore, that pretty
and attractive, but meddlesome vixen, is at the bottom of it all. Richmond will not fear Baltimore
after the rails are laid. Her prosperity will date
anew from the time of her iron wedding with Lynchburg. We shall see her merchants on our streets
again, and see them often. That will be a better day.

Alas! there are many we shall not see. John G. Meem, Sam'l McCorkle, John Robin McDaniel, John Hollins, Chas. Phelps, Jno. R. D. Payne, Jehu Williams, Ambrose Rucker, Wilson P. Bryant, (who died the other day,) and many, many others will not come to Richmond any more. They are gone. And if they came, they would not meet the men they used to meet; very few of them at least. Jacquelin P. Taylor, John N. Gordon, Thos. R. Price, Lewis D. Crenshaw, James Dunlop—why add to the list? They too are gone.

But the sons of the old-time merchants of Lynchburg will meet here the sons of the old-time merchants of Richmond, and the meeting of the two, the mingling of the waters—Blackwater creek with Bacon Quarter branch—deuce take it! I have gone off on the water line again—the admixture, I should say, of the sills of Campbell with the spikes of Henrico, the readjustment, so to speak, of the ties (R. R. ties) that bind us, will more than atone for the obsolete canal, and draw us all the closer by reason of our long separation and estrangement. Richmond and Lynchburg united will go onward and upward in a common career of glory and prosperity. And is there, can there be, a Virginian, deserving the name, who would envy that glory, or for a moment retard that prosperity? Not one, I am sure.

Allow me, now that my reminiscences are ended, allow me, as an old stager and packet-horn reverer, one last Parthian shot. It is this: If the James river does not behave better hereafter than it has done of late, the railroad will have to be suspended in mid-heaven by means of a series of stationary balloons; travelling then may be a little wabbly, but at all events, it won't be wet.

G. W. BAGBY.

www.ingramcontent.com/pod-product-compliance
Lightning Source LLC
Chambersburg PA
CBHW021449090426
42739CB00009B/1689